OCEANS ALIVE

Eels

by Derek Zobel

BELLWETHER MEDIA • MINNEAPOLIS, MN

Note to Librarians, Teachers, and Parents:

Blastoff! Readers are carefully developed by literacy experts and combine standards-based content with developmentally appropriate text.

Level 1 provides the most support through repetition of high-frequency words, light text, predictable sentence patterns, and strong visual support.

Level 2 offers early readers a bit more challenge through varied simple sentences, increased text load, and less repetition of high-frequency words.

Level 3 advances early-fluent readers toward fluency through increased text and concept load, less reliance on visuals, longer sentences, and more literary language.

Level 4 builds reading stamina by providing more text per page, increased use of punctuation, greater variation in sentence patterns, and increasingly challenging vocabulary.

Level 5 encourages children to move from "learning to read" to "reading to learn" by providing even more text, varied writing styles, and less familiar topics.

Whichever book is right for your reader, Blastoff! Readers are the perfect books to build confidence and encourage a love of reading that will last a lifetime!

This edition first published in 2008 by Bellwether Media.

No part of this publication may be reproduced in whole or in part without written permission of the publisher. For information regarding permission, write to Bellwether Media Inc., Attention: Permissions Department, Post Office Box 19349, Minneapolis, MN 55419.

Library of Congress Cataloging-in-Publication Data
Zobel, Derek, 1983–
  Eels / by Derek Zobel.
    p. cm. – (Blastoff! readers: Oceans alive)
Summary: "Simple text and full color photographs introduce beginning readers to eels. Developed by literacy experts for students in kindergarten through third grade"—Provided by publisher.
  Includes bibliographical references and index.
  ISBN-13: 978-1-60014-172-0 (hardcover : alk. paper)
  ISBN-10: 1-60014-172-2 (hardcover : alk. paper)
  1. Eels—Juvenile literature. I. Title.

QL637.9.A5Z63 2008
597'.43—dc22   2007040277

Contents

What Are Eels?   4

Parts of an Eel   10

How Eels Eat   15

Eels and Eel Pits   19

Glossary   22

To Learn More   23

Index   24

Eels are a kind of fish. Most eels live in the ocean.

Some live near the **coast** in **coral reefs**. Others live in deep water.

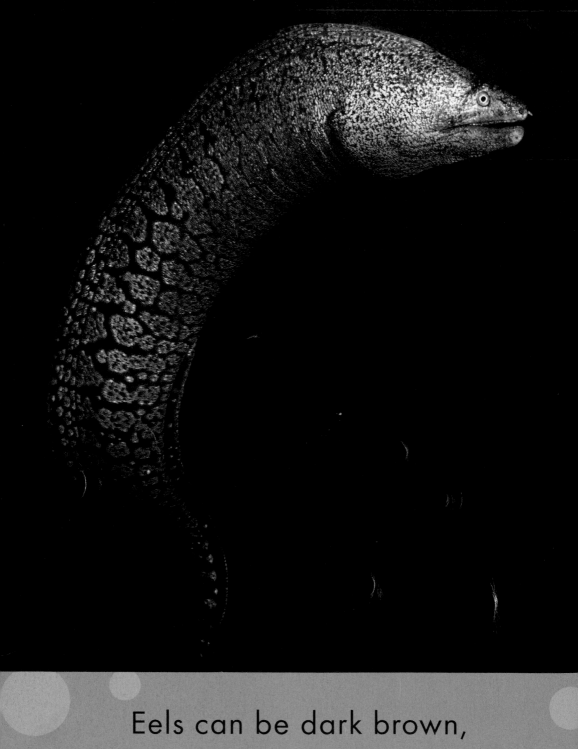

Eels can be dark brown, gray, or black.

They can also be bright
and colorful.

Eels come in many sizes. Some are longer than a person.

They move their bodies like snakes
to swim. Moving back and forth
pushes them through the water.

9

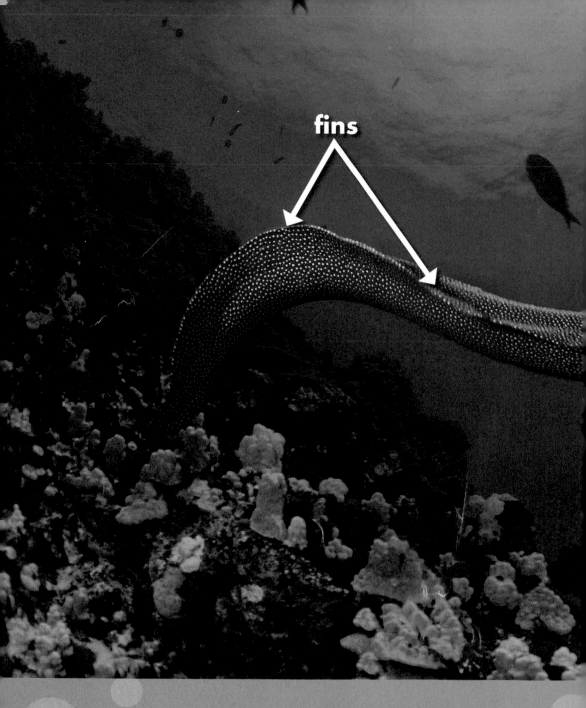

fins

Eels have long **fins** on their back. Some eels have fins on their sides.

Fins help an eel steer and stop in the water.

Eels use **gills** to breathe.
Some eels can also breathe
through their skin.

gills

Most eels do not have **scales** like other fish.

Eels have **slime** on their skin. The slime helps protect their skin from cuts and scrapes.

14

Eels have a powerful sense of smell. It helps them find food.

Eels hunt for **prey** at night. They eat fish, **crustaceans**, and other tiny animals.

Some eels use strong jaws
and sharp teeth to catch
fish and crustaceans.

Small eels catch tiny animals that drift by in the **current**.

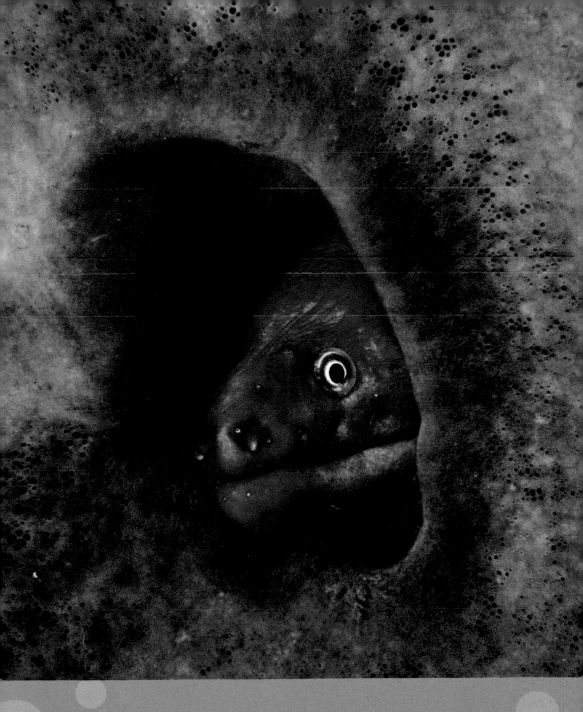

Eels can hide in holes called **eel pits**. Some eels dig their own eel pits.

Other eels find holes to use as eel pits. Some eels live in eel pits next to each other.

They hide in their eel pits to stay safe during the day.

Glossary

coast—the land along the edge of an ocean

coral reef—a structure in the ocean made from the skeletons of many small animals called corals

crustacean—a sea creature with an outer shell such as shrimp, crabs, and lobsters

current—moving water in a river or ocean

eel pits—holes in which eels hide; eels can find or dig eel pits.

fins—flaps on a fish's body; an eel uses fins to steer in the water.

gills—openings on an eel that it uses to breathe; gills move oxygen from the water to the eel's blood.

prey—an animal hunted by another animal for food

scales—small, hard plates that cover the skin of many fish

slime—a clear, slippery liquid that covers the body of an eel

To Learn More

AT THE LIBRARY

Rake, Jody Sullivan. *Eels*. Minneapolis, Minn.:
Capstone, 2006.

Stone, Lynn M. *Eels*. Vero Beach, Fla.: Rourke, 2005.

Wallace, Karen. *Think of an Eel*. Cambridge, Mass.:
Candlewick, 2004.

ON THE WEB

Learning more about eels
is as easy as 1, 2, 3.

1. Go to www.factsurfer.com

2. Enter "eels" into search box.

3. Click the "Surf" button and you will see a list of
    related web sites.

With factsurfer.com, finding more information is just a
click away.

Index

animals, 16, 18

bodies, 9

coast, 5

coral reef, 5

crustaceans, 16, 17

current, 18

cuts, 14

eel pits, 19, 20, 21

fins, 10, 11

fish, 4, 13, 16, 17

food, 15

gills, 12

hole, 19, 20

jaws, 17

ocean, 4

person, 8

prey, 16

scales, 13

scrapes, 14

sense of smell, 15

skin, 12, 14

slime, 14

snakes, 9

teeth, 17